THE PASTA COOKBOOK

Edited by
Carole Handslip

Contents

This edition first published 1979 by
Octopus Books Limited
59 Grosvenor Street, London W.1.

© 1979 Octopus Books Limited

ISBN 0 7064 1064 5

Produced and printed in Hong Kong by
Mandarin Publishers Limited
22a Westlands Road, Quarry Bay

Frontispiece: PASTA SHAPES
(Photograph: Pasta Information Centre)

Weights and Measures

All measurements in this book are based on Imperial weights and measures, with American equivalents given in parenthesis.

Measurements in *weight* in the Imperial and American system are the same. Liquid measurements are different, and the following table shows the equivalents:

Liquid measurements
1 Imperial pint .... 20 fluid ounces
1 American pint .... 16 fluid ounces
1 American cup .... 8 fluid ounces

Level spoon measurements are used in all the recipes.

Spoon measurements
1 tablespoon (1T) .... 15 ml
1 teaspoon .... 5 ml

ITALIAN PASTA

1. RIGATONI — These are ridged tubes, suitable for a main course with a meat sauce.

2. ANELLINI — Used with a sauce or in soups, anellini are always popular with children.

3. RUOTE — Shaped like wheels, ruote can be used in robust soups or with a sauce.

4. TRIPOLINE — Wide, ribbon-like pasta, this is used like spaghetti with a sauce.

5. VERMICELLI — Obtainable in nests or in lengths like spaghetti, vermicelli is usually used in clear soups.

6. LINGUINE — This is a narrow, flat ribbon pasta used like spaghetti.

7. TAGLIATELLE and FETTUCCINE — These two are very similar; they may be coiled or straight and the so called 'verde' or green pasta is achieved by flavouring with spinach.

8. RAVIOLI — These are little squares of pasta containing a savoury filling.

9. TORTELLINI — Tortellini are twisted into a shape rather like a croissant with the ends joined together. These little rounds of pasta are filled with a savoury mixture.

10. SPAGHETTI — The most popular of all kinds of pasta, spaghetti is used as a first or main course with a sauce.

11. FARFALLE — Bow-shaped pasta, farfalle is used with a sauce for a main course.

12. FARFALLINE — This miniature farfalle is used in soups.

13. TORTIGLIONE — These spirals of pasta are suitable to serve with a sauce for a main course.

14. PENNE — This is short cut macaroni with the ends cut diagonally. It is obtainable in several sizes.

15. CONCHIGLIE — Pasta shells are obtainable in 3 sizes – small, medium and large.

16. CANNELLONI — These tubes of pasta are served stuffed with a meat or other savoury filling.

17. LUMACHE — Lumache are small snail shells of pasta.

18. SEME CICORIA — Pasta seeds are usually cooked in soups.

19. STELLETTE — These very small star shapes are used in soups.

20. DITALI — Ditali are small tubes of pasta, used in robust soups such as minestrone.

21. DITALINI — These are tiny tubes, also used in soups.

HOMEMADE PASTA

Homemade Egg Pasta

3 eggs
4 tablespoons (¼ cup) water
1 teaspoon salt

1 lb. (4 cups) plain (all-purpose)
flour

Break the eggs into a large mixing bowl, add the water, salt and about a quarter of the flour. Beat the mixture until smooth, then add the remaining flour and mix to a dough, using your hands. Turn the dough onto a floured surface and knead well for 10 minutes until smooth and elastic, then cover with a damp cloth and leave to rest for 20 minutes.

Divide the dough in half and roll out into very thin sheets, turning frequently on the rolling pin and flouring the paste each time to prevent it sticking. When it has been stretched sufficiently it will be almost transparent. Lay the first sheet of paste on a clean cloth while rolling out the second half.

10

Tagliatelle

Dust the pasta well with flour, then roll up loosely and cut into ¼ inch strips. Gently unroll with a tossing movement to prevent the strips sticking together. Spread on a clean cloth to dry for about 30 minutes, before cooking in boiling salted water for 4-6 minutes.

Lasagne

Dust the pasta well with flour and roll up loosely. Cut into 2 inch strips and dry for about 30 minutes before cooking. Drop a few at a time into boiling salted water and cook for 4-6 minutes. Remove the lasagne and drop into cold water, then drain and use as required.

Cannelloni

Cut the pasta sheet into rectangles 3 × 4 inches and dry for about 30 minutes before cooking. Drop into boiling salted water, a few at a time, and boil for 4-6 minutes. Remove the cannelloni and drop into cold water, then drain and use as required.

How to Cook Pasta

1 lb. of pasta serves 4 people for a main course, or 6 people for a first course.

Use a large saucepan which will hold 8 pints (9 pints) of water for 1 lb. of pasta. Bring the pan of water to the boil, then add 1 tablespoon of salt. Throw the pasta shapes into the boiling water, all at the same time, and stir to prevent them sticking. If using long pasta, coil it into the boiling water as it softens until the whole length is covered. Stir frequently with a wooden spoon or fork to prevent the pasta from sticking. The cooking time varies with the shape and thickness of the pasta, but as a general rule spaghetti will take 12-15 minutes, short cut shapes a little less. 'Pasta fatta in casa' or homemade pasta, will take only 4-6 minutes to cook.

To test whether it is ready, lift out one piece with a fork and bite; it should be 'al dente', which is soft but with a slight resistance in the centre. When cooked, drain in a colander to remove as much water as possible and place in a heated dish.

Pasta should be eaten as soon as it has been prepared, if it is to be served hot, and is improved by the addition of a pat of butter on the top, or a little olive oil stirred into it.

SOUPS

Vermicelli and Bean Soup

8 oz. (1 cup) red kidney beans,
  soaked overnight and drained
3 pints (7½ cups) water
4 tablespoons (¼ cup) tomato purée
2 tablespoons olive oil
1 onion, chopped
1 clove garlic, crushed
3 sticks celery, chopped
3 carrots, sliced

2 tomatoes, peeled and chopped
2 tablespoons chopped fresh parsley
1 teaspoon dried oregano
salt
freshly ground black pepper
4 oz. (1 cup) vermicelli, broken
  into short lengths
grated Parmesan cheese to serve

Place the beans in a large pan with the water and the tomato purée,
bring to the boil, cover and simmer for 1½ hours. Heat the oil in a
separate pan and fry the onion and garlic until transparent. Add the
celery and carrots and fry for a further 5 minutes. Add these
vegetables to the beans with the tomatoes, parsley, oregano, salt and
pepper; cover and simmer for 20 minutes. Add the vermicelli and
cook until tender. Serve sprinkled with the Parmesan cheese.
Serves 6-8

VERMICELLI AND BEAN SOUP
(Photograph: Pasta Information Centre)

Minestrone with Garlic Sauce

4 oz. (½ cup) haricot (navy)
  beans, soaked overnight and
  drained
3 tablespoons olive oil
1 onion, chopped
8 oz. (1½ cups) courgettes
  (zucchini), chopped
4 tomatoes, peeled and chopped
4 oz. (1 cup) mushrooms, sliced
8 oz. (2 cups) French (green)
  beans, cut into ½ inch lengths

4 oz. cauliflower, divided into
  florets
½ small cabbage, shredded
3 pints (7½ cups) water
salt and pepper
2 oz. (½ cup) vermicelli, broken
  into short lengths
2 tablespoons pesto (see page 62)
grated Parmesan cheese to serve

Cook the beans in boiling water for 1½ hours or until tender, adding salt towards the end of the cooking time.

Heat the oil in a pan and fry the onion until soft. Add the remaining vegetables, water, salt and pepper and simmer for 30–40 minutes. Add the pasta and haricot (navy) beans and cook for a further 4–5 minutes. Just before serving stir in the pesto. Serve with Parmesan cheese handed separately.
Serves 6-8

Vermicelli and Lentil Soup

2 tablespoons oil
1 onion, chopped
2 oz. (3 slices) bacon, chopped
2 sticks celery, chopped
2 carrots, chopped
4 oz. (½ cup) green lentils
1 tablespoon chopped fresh parsley

1 teaspoon chopped fresh mint
1 tablespoon tomato purée
2½ pints (6¼ cups) chicken stock
salt
freshly ground black pepper
2 oz. (½ cup) vermicelli, broken
  into short lengths

Heat the oil in a pan and fry the onion and bacon for 3 minutes. Add the remaining ingredients, except the vermicelli, and simmer gently for 1 hour, until the lentils are tender. Add the pasta and cook for a further 10 minutes. Adjust the seasoning and serve.
Serves 6

Fish Soup

2 lb. assorted fish (mackerel, cod, grey mullet), cleaned
3 pints (7½ cups) water
salt and pepper
bay leaf
3 tablespoons olive oil
1 onion, chopped
2 cloves garlic, crushed
3 sticks celery, chopped
1 leek, sliced
2 tablespoons chopped fresh parsley
1 lb. (2 cups) tomatoes, peeled and chopped
1 tablespoon tomato purée
2 pints (5 cups) mussels
¼ pint (⅔ cup) white wine
2 oz. (½ cup) vermicelli, broken into short lengths
chopped fresh parsley to garnish

Remove the heads and tails from the fish and fillet them. Place all the trimmings in a pan with the water, salt and bay leaf and simmer for 30 minutes. Strain and reserve the stock.

Heat the oil in a pan, add the onion and garlic and fry until soft. Add the celery, leek, parsley, seasoning to taste, tomatoes, tomato purée and the reserved fish stock and simmer gently for 15 minutes. Cut the fish into chunks, add to the pan and simmer gently for 10 minutes.

Scrub the mussels, remove the beards, then rinse well to remove all grit. Discard any that will not close when tapped. Place in a pan with the wine and cook briskly for 5-7 minutes, shaking the pan occasionally until the shells open. Discard any mussels that do not open. Shell the mussels and add to the soup with the cooking juices and the vermicelli. Simmer for 4-5 minutes and serve sprinkled with the parsley.

Serves 6-8

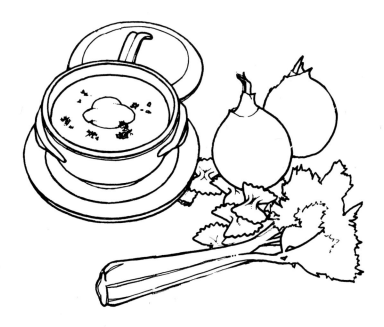

Watercress and Vermicelli Soup

2 tablespoons oil
2 onions, sliced
2 bunches watercress, roughly
 chopped
2½ pints (6¼ cups) chicken stock
salt

freshly ground black pepper
3 oz. (¾ cup) vermicelli, broken
 into short lengths
1 egg, hard-boiled and finely
 chopped

Heat the oil in a pan and fry the onion and watercress gently for 5
minutes, then add the stock, salt and pepper and simmer for 20
minutes. Throw in the vermicelli and simmer for a further 5
minutes. Serve with the chopped hard-boiled egg.
Serves 4-6

Stuffed Pasta in Broth

2 tablespoons oil
12 oz. (1½ cups) lean pork,
 chopped
1 onion, chopped
1 stick celery, chopped
2 fl. oz. (¼ cup) sherry
1 egg
2 oz. (½ cup) grated Parmesan
 cheese

salt
freshly ground black pepper
pinch of ground nutmeg
½ quantity egg pasta dough (see
 page 10)
3 pints (7½ cups) chicken stock
2 oz. (½ cup) grated Parmesan
 cheese

Heat the oil in a pan and fry the pork, onion and celery for 5
minutes. Add the sherry and simmer, covered, for a further 20
minutes. Mince (grind) the meat mixture, then add the egg, cheese,
salt, pepper and nutmeg and allow to cool.
  Roll out the dough into a thin sheet and cut in half. Brush one
piece with cold water and place small heaps of the stuffing at regular
intervals on the paste. Cover with the second sheet of paste. Press
down round each mound of filling, then cut into 1½ inch rounds
using a pastry wheel or small fluted cutter. Bring the chicken stock
to the boil. Carefully drop the cappelletti into the boiling stock and
cook for about 4 minutes until they rise to the top. Serve in soup
plates with the stock and Parmesan cheese.
Serves 6

WATERCRESS AND VERMICELLI SOUP
(Photograph: Pasta Information Centre)

Cream Cheese and Tomato Soup

3 tablespoons oil
1 onion, sliced
1 clove garlic, crushed
1 lb. (2 cups) tomatoes, peeled and
  chopped
2 tablespoons tomato purée

1 teaspoon sugar
2 pints (5 cups) chicken stock
salt and pepper
2 oz. (½ cup) vermicelli, broken
  into short lengths
4 oz. (½ cup) cream cheese

Heat the oil in a pan and fry the onion and garlic until soft. Add the tomatoes, tomato purée, sugar, stock and seasoning, bring to the boil and simmer gently for 30 minutes. Add the pasta and continue cooking for 4-5 minutes until tender. Add the cream cheese in small pieces and stir until dissolved. Serve immediately.
Serves 4-6

Spinach and Vermicelli Soup

1½ oz. (3 T) butter
1 onion, chopped
½ pint (1¼ cups) spinach purée
1½ pints (3¾ cups) stock

salt and pepper
2 oz. (½ cup) vermicelli, broken
  into short lengths
grated rind and juice of 1 lemon

Heat the butter in a pan, add the onion and cook for 5 minutes or until soft. Add the spinach, stock and seasoning to taste and simmer gently for 15 minutes. Add the vermicelli and the lemon rind and juice and simmer for a further 4-5 minutes or until the pasta is cooked. If liked, serve with croûtons.
Serves 4

Chicken Liver Soup

1 oz. (2 T) butter
1 onion, chopped
1 clove garlic, crushed
4 oz. (½ cup) chicken livers,
   chopped
12 oz. (2¼ cups) peas

2 pints (5 cups) chicken stock
2 oz. (¼ cup) stellette (stars)
salt and pepper
2 teaspoons chopped fresh parsley
2 tablespoons grated Parmesan
   cheese

Heat the butter in a pan, add the onion and garlic and cook for 5 minutes or until soft. Add the livers and fry for 3 minutes, stirring, until browned. Add the peas, stock, pasta and salt and pepper to taste. Bring to the boil and simmer very gently for 12 minutes or until the pasta is 'al dente'.

   Stir in the parsley and cheese and serve immediately.
Serves 4-6

Minestrone with Bacon and Herbs

4 oz. (½ cup) haricot (navy)
   beans, soaked overnight and
   drained
3 tablespoons oil
2 onions, chopped
2 cloves garlic, crushed
4 slices streaky (fatty) bacon,
   chopped
3 pints (7½ cups) water
4 tomatoes, peeled and chopped
2 tablespoons chopped fresh parsley
1 teaspoon chopped fresh thyme

1 teaspoon chopped fresh basil
2 carrots, chopped
2 potatoes, chopped
1 stick celery, chopped
1 leek, chopped
½ small cabbage, shredded
salt
freshly ground black pepper
2 oz. (¼ cup) small pasta shells
2 tablespoons grated Parmesan
   cheese

Cook the beans in plenty of simmering water for 1½ hours, adding salt toward the end of cooking. When the beans are tender, drain them well.

   Heat the oil in a pan and cook the onions and garlic until transparent, add the bacon and fry for a further 2-3 minutes. Add the water, beans, tomatoes, herbs, carrots, potatoes, celery, leek, cabbage, salt and pepper to taste. Cover and simmer for 30 minutes, then add the pasta and cook for 20 minutes, or until the pasta is tender. Stir in the Parmesan cheese and serve immediately. Serve with extra Parmesan cheese handed separately.
Serves 6-8

Beef Broth with Pasta

2 lb. shin of beef, cut into cubes
1 veal bone
4 pints (10 cups) water
2 onions
2 sticks celery
1 carrot

2 sprigs parsley
1 tablespoon salt
2 oz. (½ cup) small pasta shapes
 e.g. ditali
chopped fresh parsley to garnish

Place all the ingredients, except the pasta and chopped parsley, in a large saucepan, bring to the boil and remove the scum. Simmer gently for 3-4 hours to make a strong stock. Strain, cool and leave in the refrigerator overnight.

Remove the fat from the surface. Place the stock in a pan and bring to the boil, add the pasta and simmer for 7-10 minutes or until the pasta is cooked. Sprinkle with parsley and serve.
Serves 8-10

Bean and Mushroom Soup

4 oz. (½ cup) haricot (navy)
 beans, soaked overnight and
 drained
4 oz. (½ cup) red kidney beans,
 soaked overnight and drained
2 tablespoons oil
1 onion, sliced
1 clove garlic, crushed
4 oz. (1 cup) button mushrooms,
 sliced

2 pints (5 cups) beef stock
6 oz. (1¼ cups) broad (lima)
 beans, shelled
salt and pepper
2 oz. (generous ½ cup) pasta rings
Garnish (optional):
4 slices streaky (fatty) bacon,
 crisply grilled (broiled) and
 chopped
1 tablespoon chopped fresh parsley

Place the haricot (navy) and red kidney beans in separate pans, cover with cold water and bring to the boil. Simmer the haricot (navy) beans for 1½ hours and the kidney beans for 1 hour or until tender, adding salt towards the end of cooking.

Heat the oil in a pan and fry the onion until soft, then add the garlic, mushrooms, stock, broad (lima) beans and seasoning to taste. Simmer for 10 minutes. Add the pasta rings and the drained beans and simmer for a further 15 minutes or until the pasta is tender. Serve sprinkled with the bacon and parsley.
Serves 6

BEAN AND MUSHROOM SOUP
(Photograph: Pasta Information Centre)

Meatball and Noodle Soup

8 oz. (1 cup) minced (ground) beef
1 onion, finely chopped
½ teaspoon ground cinnamon
salt
freshly ground black pepper
2 pints (5 cups) water
2 oz. (¼ cup) dried peas, soaked
  overnight and drained

2 oz. (¼ cup) lentils
4 spring onions (scallions), chopped
2 tablespoons chopped fresh parsley
4 oz. (1 cup) egg noodles
1 tablespoon chopped fresh mint to
  garnish

Place the beef, onion, cinnamon, salt and pepper in a bowl and mix together well. Shape into small balls, the size of a walnut, and set aside.

Put the water in a large pan with the peas and lentils, bring to the boil and simmer for 20 minutes. Add the meatballs, spring onions (scallions), salt, pepper and parsley and simmer again for 20 minutes. Stir in the noodles and simmer for a further 15 minutes, adding a little more water if too thick.

Sprinkle with the mint and serve hot.
Serves 4

Green Minestrone

4 oz. (½ cup) haricot (navy) beans, soaked overnight and drained
2 tablespoons olive oil
2 leeks, sliced
1 clove garlic, crushed
2 tablespoons chopped fresh parsley
2 tablespoons mixed chopped fresh herbs

3 pints (7½ cups) water
2 sticks celery, chopped
4 tomatoes, peeled and chopped
2 potatoes, diced
salt and pepper
2 oz. (½ cup) ditali or other small pasta
4 oz. (¾ cup) peas
grated Parmesan cheese to serve

Cook the beans in boiling water for 1½ hours or until tender, adding the salt towards the end of the cooking time.

Heat the oil in a pan and fry the leeks, garlic and half the parsley and herbs for 10 minutes. Add the water, celery, tomatoes, potatoes and seasoning and simmer for 30 minutes. Add the pasta, peas and haricot (navy) beans and simmer for a further 15 minutes until the pasta is cooked and the vegetables tender. Stir in the remaining parsley and herbs and serve with Parmesan cheese handed separately.

Serves 6-8

Mushroom and Pasta Chowder

2 tablespoons oil
1 onion, chopped
6 slices bacon, chopped
1 tablespoon flour
1 pint (2½ cups) stock
½ pint (1¼ cups) milk

2 oz. (1 generous cup) pasta wheels
1 clove garlic, crushed
4 oz. (1 cup) button mushrooms, sliced
salt and pepper

Heat the oil in a pan and fry the onion and bacon gently for 4-5 minutes until soft. Stir in the flour and cook for 1 minute. Gradually pour in the stock and mix well to blend. Bring to the boil, stirring continuously. Add the milk, pasta, garlic, mushrooms and seasoning and simmer gently for 20 minutes or until the pasta is cooked.

Serve with crusty bread.

Serves 4

FIRST COURSES AND QUICK DISHES

Green and Yellow Noodles

8 oz. (2 cups) green noodles
8 oz. (2 cups) plain noodles
2 tablespoons oil
2 cloves garlic, crushed
½ pint (1¼ cups) double (heavy)
  cream

2 tablespoons chopped fresh parsley
1 teaspoon dried oregano
1 oz. (2 T) butter
2 oz. (½ cup) grated Parmesan
  cheese

Cook the noodles in boiling salted water until 'al dente', then drain well.

Heat the oil in a pan, add the garlic and fry for 1 minute, then add the cream and the herbs and simmer very gently for 2-3 minutes. Mix the cream sauce with the noodles and stir in the butter and cheese. Transfer to a heated dish and serve at once.

Serves 6

GREEN AND YELLOW NOODLES
(Photograph: Princes-Buitoni)

Buttered Tagliatelle

1 lb. tagliatelle
4 oz. (½ cup) butter, cut into
  pieces
3 oz. (¾ cup) grated Parmesan
  cheese

salt
freshly ground black pepper

Cook the tagliatelle in boiling salted water until 'al dente', then pour off most of the water, leaving sufficient to moisten the pasta. Add the butter, cheese, salt and pepper. Stir gently and leave for 1-2 minutes to melt.
    Serve extra butter and cheese separately.
Serves 6

Tagliatelle with Cream Cheese and Nuts

1 oz. (2 T) butter
12 oz. (1½ cups) cream cheese
2 oz. (½ cup) grated Parmesan
  cheese

4 oz. (1 cup) walnuts, coarsely
  chopped
1 tablespoon chopped fresh parsley
1 lb. tagliatelle verde

Heat the butter in a pan, add the cream cheese and heat very gently, without boiling, until melted. Add the Parmesan cheese, walnuts and parsley and heat through.
    Cook the tagliatelle in boiling salted water until 'al dente', drain and mix with the cheese sauce. Add seasoning, if liked. Pour into a heated serving dish and serve with extra Parmesan cheese.
Serves 6

Tortellini with Cheese Filling

12 oz. (3 cups) Ricotta cheese
2 oz. (½ cup) grated Parmesan
  cheese
2 tablespoons chopped fresh parsley
1 egg

salt
freshly ground black pepper
pinch of ground nutmeg
1 quantity egg pasta dough (see
  page 10)

Place the Ricotta, Parmesan, parsley, egg, salt, pepper and nutmeg in a bowl and mix together well.

Roll out the dough very thinly and cut into 2 inch rounds. Place about ½ teaspoon of the filling on each circle and fold over so that the one edge is a little short of the other edge. Bring the two ends together, curling the tortellini round the finger, and press them together firmly to form a ring.

Place the tortellini on a floured tray and allow them to dry for about 30 minutes, then cook them in boiling salted water for about 4 minutes until they rise to the top. Remove from the pan and serve with melted butter and Parmesan cheese.
Serves 6

Tortellini with Cream Sauce

Prepare the tortellini as above and cook them in boiling salted water for 4 minutes, then drain. Heat ½ pint (1¼ cups) double (heavy) cream gently, add the tortellini and season well with salt and freshly ground black pepper. Serve at once.

Spaghetti with Garlic and Chilli

4 fl. oz. (½ cup) olive oil
4 cloves garlic, finely chopped
1 red chilli, seeded and chopped

1 lb. spaghetti
2 tablespoons chopped fresh parsley
freshly ground black pepper

Heat the oil in a pan with the garlic and chilli and fry for 1-2 minutes.

Cook the spaghetti in boiling salted water until 'al dente', drain and mix with the oil mixture and the parsley. Season with black pepper and serve immediately.
Serves 6

Spaghetti Carbonara

1 lb. spaghetti
1 tablespoon olive oil
6 oz. (¾ cup) lean bacon, chopped
2 fl. oz. (¼ cup) single (light)
  cream
2 eggs, beaten
2 oz. (½ cup) grated Parmesan
  cheese

salt
freshly ground black pepper
pinch of cayenne pepper
1½ oz. (3 T) butter, cut into small
  pieces

Cook the spaghetti in boiling salted water until 'al dente'.
Meanwhile, heat the oil in a small frying pan (skillet) and fry the
bacon until crisp.
   Mix the cream, eggs and cheese and season to taste with salt,
pepper and cayenne. Drain the spaghetti and toss in the butter over a
moderate heat until it has melted. Stir in the bacon, then the egg
mixture and toss until the spaghetti is thoroughly coated. Serve
immediately.
Serves 4

Fettuccine with Truffles

1 lb. fettuccine
2 oz. (¼ cup) butter
2 egg yolks
½ pint (1¼ cups) double (heavy)
  cream
2 oz. (½ cup) grated Parmesan
  cheese

salt
freshly ground black pepper
small can white truffles, drained
  and sliced

Cook the fettuccine in boiling salted water until 'al dente', then drain
well.
   Heat together the butter, egg yolks, cream and cheese, stirring
constantly, until just beginning to thicken. Add the noodles, season
well with salt and pepper and place in a heated serving dish. Sprinkle
over the truffles and serve with extra Parmesan cheese.
Serves 4-6

Pasta Shells with Walnut Sauce

2 oz. (½ cup) walnuts
1½ -2 oz. (1-1½ cups) chopped
  fresh parsley
1 teaspoon sea salt
2 oz. (¼ cup) butter, softened

2 tablespoons fresh breadcrumbs
4 tablespoons (¼ cup) olive oil
2 tablespoons double (heavy) cream
freshly ground black pepper
1 lb. (8 cups) large pasta shells

Pour boiling water over the walnuts and soak for 2-3 minutes, then skin them. Pound the walnuts, parsley and salt in a mortar until reduced to a paste. Beat in the butter and the breadcrumbs, then gradually add the oil until it is a thick paste. Stir in the cream and season with black pepper.

Cook the pasta shells in boiling salted water until 'al dente'. Drain the pasta, mix with the walnut sauce and heat through for 1-2 minutes.
Serves 6

Tagliatelle with Mushrooms and Cream Sauce

3 tablespoons oil
1 small onion, chopped
1 clove garlic, crushed
8 oz. (2 cups) mushrooms, sliced
4 oz. (½ cup) prosciutto ham,
  shredded

½ pint (1¼ cups) single (light)
  cream
salt
freshly ground black pepper
1 lb. tagliatelle

Heat the oil in a pan and fry the onion and garlic until transparent. Add the mushrooms and ham and cook for a further 5 minutes. Stir in the cream, season with salt and pepper, and heat gently for 5 minutes.

Cook the tagliatelle in boiling salted water until 'al dente', then drain. Mix with the cream sauce and transfer to a heated serving dish.
Serves 4-6

Tagliatelle Omelette

6 eggs
4 tablespoons (¼ cup) grated
 Parmesan cheese
salt and pepper
8 oz. cooked tagliatelle, coarsely
 chopped

2 tablespoons olive oil
6 oz. Mozzarella cheese, thinly
 sliced

Beat the eggs with the Parmesan cheese and seasoning, add the
tagliatelle and mix well. Heat the oil in a large frying pan (skillet) and
pour in half the noodle mixture. Arrange the Mozzarella on top, then
cover with the remaining noodle mixture.

Fry over moderate heat until brown underneath and lightly set.
Then turn the omelette onto a plate and slide back into the pan to
brown the other side. Turn onto a hot serving dish, cut into wedges
and serve immediately.
Serves 3-4

Mortadella Omelette

8 eggs
salt and pepper
6 oz. cooked tagliatelle, roughly
 chopped
8 oz. Mortadella, cut into cubes

4 tablespoons (¼ cup) grated
 Parmesan cheese
2 tablespoons chopped fresh parsley
3 tablespoons oil

Beat the eggs together with the seasoning, then add the noodles,
Mortadella, Parmesan and parsley. Heat the oil in a frying pan
(skillet) and pour in a quarter of the egg mixture. Fry over a
moderate heat until brown underneath and lightly set. Then turn the
omelette onto a plate and slide back into the pan to brown the other
side. Keep warm. Cook the remaining mixture in the same way.
Serve with a green salad.
Serves 4

MEAT

Spaghetti with Bacon and Tomato Sauce

2 tablespoons oil
1 onion, chopped
6 oz. piece of bacon, cut into strips
1 lb. (2 cups) tomatoes, peeled and
  chopped
1 tablespoon chopped fresh parsley

salt
freshly ground black pepper
1 lb. spaghetti
2 oz. (½ cup) Pecorino cheese,
  grated

Heat the oil in a pan and fry the onion and bacon for 5 minutes. Add the tomatoes, parsley, salt and pepper and cook for a further 5-10 minutes.

Cook the spaghetti in boiling salted water until 'al dente', drain well and add the sauce and the cheese. Stir once and serve on a heated serving dish.
Serves 4-6

Spaghetti with Ham and Peas

2 tablespoons olive oil
4 oz. (½ cup) prosciutto ham,
  chopped
1 onion, chopped
1 clove garlic, crushed
1 lb. (2 cups) tomatoes, peeled and
  chopped

½ pint (1¼ cups) stock
2 tablespoons tomato purée
1 tablespoon chopped fresh parsley
8 oz. (1½ cups) peas
salt and pepper
1 lb. spaghetti

Heat the oil in a saucepan, add the ham, onion and garlic and fry gently for 7 minutes or until the onion is lightly golden. Add the tomatoes, stock, tomato purée, parsley, peas and salt and pepper to taste and bring to the boil. Reduce the heat and simmer for 30 minutes.

Meanwhile, cook the spaghetti in a large pan of boiling salted water for 10–12 minutes or until 'al dente'. Drain thoroughly and transfer to a warm serving dish. Add the sauce, toss well and serve immediately.

Serves 4

Spaghetti with Hare Sauce

½ hare
2 tablespoons oil
1 onion, chopped
4 slices bacon, chopped
2 cloves garlic, crushed
4 oz. (1 cup) button mushrooms,
 sliced
1 tablespoon tomato purée

¼ pint (⅔ cup) red wine
½ pint (1 ¼ cups) stock
1 tablespoon chopped fresh parsley
½ teaspoon dried oregano
salt and pepper
1 lb. spaghetti
2 oz. (½ cup) grated Parmesan
 cheese

Cut all the hare meat off the bones and chop fairly finely. Heat the oil in a pan and fry the onion and bacon for 6-7 minutes or until golden. Add the hare meat, garlic, mushrooms, tomato purée, wine, stock, herbs and seasoning to taste. Simmer gently for 1 hour or until the hare is tender and the mixture fairly thick.

Cook the spaghetti in boiling salted water for 10-12 minutes or until 'al dente'. Drain and stir in the Parmesan cheese. Place in a serving dish and pour over the hare sauce.

Serves 4-6

Spaghetti with Creamy Chicken Sauce

12 oz. spaghetti
3 oz. (⅓ cup) butter
2 oz. (½ cup) flour
¾ pint (2 cups) chicken stock
¼ pint (⅔ cup) single (light)
 cream
2 tablespoons sherry

salt and pepper
4 oz. (1 cup) mushrooms, sliced
12 oz. (1 ½ cups) cooked chicken,
 cut into cubes
parsley sprigs to garnish
grated Parmesan cheese to serve

Cook the spaghetti in a large pan of boiling salted water until 'al dente'. Drain and set aside.

Melt 2 oz. (¼ cup) of the butter in a pan, stir in the flour and cook for 1 minute. Gradually pour in the stock and mix until smooth. Bring to the boil, stirring constantly, and cook for 3 minutes. Mix in the cream, sherry and seasoning. Add half the sauce to the spaghetti and heat through.

Fry the mushrooms in the remaining butter for 3 minutes or until soft, and add to the remaining sauce with the chicken.

Arrange the spaghetti in a serving dish and pile the chicken mixture in the centre. Garnish with parsley and serve with Parmesan cheese handed separately.

Serves 4

Spaghetti with Bolognese Sauce

1 lb. spaghetti
Bolognese sauce:
2 tablespoons oil
2 oz. (3 slices) unsmoked bacon,
  chopped
1 onion, chopped
1 carrot, chopped
1 stick celery, chopped
8 oz. (1 cup) minced (ground) beef
4 oz. (½ cup) chicken livers, finely
  chopped

4 fl. oz. (½ cup) white wine
½ pint (1¼ cups) beef stock
2 tablespoons tomato purée
salt
freshly ground black pepper
pinch of ground nutmeg
¼ pint (⅔ cup) double (heavy)
  cream
To serve:
knob of butter
grated Parmesan cheese

Heat the oil in a pan and fry the bacon for 2 minutes, then add the onion, carrot and celery and cook for a further 5 minutes. Add the beef to the pan and cook until browned, stirring occasionally. Add the chicken livers and cook for 3 minutes, then add the remaining ingredients, except the cream. Simmer, covered, for 30–40 minutes. Just before serving, stir in the cream and heat through.

Cook the spaghetti in boiling salted water until 'al dente', drain, and mix with the sauce. Place on a heated serving dish, top with a knob of butter and serve with grated Parmesan cheese handed separately.
Serves 4–6

CAULIFLOWER AND SPAGHETTI SOUFFLÉ *(page 63)*
(Photograph: Pasta Information Centre)

Spaghetti with Kidney and Liver

2 tablespoons oil
1 onion, chopped
4 lambs' kidneys, skinned, cored
  and sliced
2 chicken livers, chopped
1 clove garlic, crushed
1 tablespoon flour
8 fl. oz. (1 cup) stock
4 oz. (1 cup) button mushrooms,
  sliced

8 oz. (1 cup) tomatoes, peeled and
  chopped
1 tablespoon chopped fresh parsley
¼ pint (⅔ cup) red wine
salt and pepper
1 lb. spaghetti
chopped fresh parsley to garnish

Heat the oil in a frying pan (skillet) and cook the onion until soft.
Add the kidneys, livers and garlic and fry for 5 minutes. Stir in the
flour and cook for 1 minute. Add the stock and bring to the boil,
stirring constantly.

Add the mushrooms, tomatoes, parsley, wine and seasoning.
Cover and simmer for 20 minutes. Cook the spaghetti in a large pan
of boiling salted water until 'al dente'. Drain and place on a heated
serving dish. Pour the kidney mixture into the centre and sprinkle
over the parsley.

Serves 4-6

Savoury Macaroni

3 tablespoons olive oil
2 cloves garlic, crushed
1 medium onion, chopped
1 red pepper, seeded and chopped
8 slices streaky (fatty) bacon
1 × 14 oz. can tomatoes
2 tablespoons chopped fresh parsley
½ teaspoon dried basil
salt and pepper
12 oz. (3 cups) penne
3 oz. (¾ cup) grated Provolone or
 Parmesan cheese

Heat 2 tablespoons of the oil in a saucepan and fry the garlic and onion for 5 minutes or until soft. Add the pepper and bacon and cook for a further 10 minutes, stirring occasionally. Add the tomatoes and the juice, parsley, basil, salt and pepper to taste and bring to the boil. Cover the pan and simmer for 20 minutes.

Cook the pasta in a large pan of boiling salted water for 8-10 minutes or until 'al dente'. Drain thoroughly. Pour the remaining oil into a hot serving dish and put in alternate layers of pasta, sauce and cheese, finishing with a layer of cheese.

Serve immediately, or cover and leave in a cool oven, 300°F, Gas Mark 2 for 10 minutes.
Serves 4

Cannelloni with Beef and Spinach

1 lb. cannelloni tubes, or 1 quantity
 egg pasta dough (see page 10), cut
 into cannelloni
2 tablespoons oil
1 onion, chopped
1 clove garlic, crushed
1 lb. (2 cups) minced (ground) beef
1 lb. spinach, cooked and chopped
1 egg
3 oz. (¾ cup) grated Parmesan
 cheese
½ teaspoon dried oregano
salt
freshly ground black pepper
1 oz. (2 T) butter
¼ pint (⅔ cup) chicken stock

Cook the cannelloni in boiling salted water until 'al dente', drain and cool slightly.

Heat the oil in a pan and cook the onion and garlic until transparent. Add the beef and cook for a further 10 minutes until brown, stirring occasionally. Mix the meat mixture with the spinach, egg, 1 oz. (¼ cup) of the Parmesan cheese, the oregano, salt and pepper until well blended.

Place a spoonful of this filling in each cannelloni tube, or place a spoonful on each square of homemade pasta and roll up. Place them side by side in a buttered ovenproof dish. Dot the butter over the cannelloni and sprinkle with the remaining cheese. Pour in the stock and bake in a moderate oven, 350°F, Gas Mark 4 for 30 minutes until browned on top.
Serves 4-6

Cannelloni with Pork and Tomato

2 tablespoons oil
1 small onion, finely chopped
1 clove garlic, crushed
1 lb. minced (ground) pork
2 tomatoes, peeled, seeded and
  chopped
2 tablespoons breadcrumbs
2 oz. (½ cup) grated Parmesan
  cheese
1 tablespoon chopped fresh parsley
2 tablespoons tomato purée
1 egg, lightly beaten

salt and pepper
1 lb. cannelloni tubes, or 1 quantity
  egg pasta dough (see page 10), cut
  into cannelloni
Sauce:
1½ oz. (3 T) butter
1½ oz. (⅓ cup) flour
¾ pint (2 cups) milk
pinch of grated nutmeg
2 oz. (½ cup) grated Parmesan
  cheese

Heat the oil, add the onion and garlic and cook for 5 minutes or until soft. Add the pork and brown on all sides. Stir in the tomatoes, breadcrumbs, cheese, parsley, tomato purée, egg and salt and pepper to taste and cook, stirring, for 3 minutes. Cool.

For the sauce, melt the butter, stir in the flour and cook for 1 minute. Gradually add the milk, stirring constantly, to make a smooth sauce. Season and add nutmeg to taste. Bring to the boil, stirring, and cook for 2 minutes. Keep warm.

Cook the pasta in a large pan of boiling salted water for 5-8 minutes or until 'al dente'. Lift out the pasta and lay, side by side, on a cloth to drain.

Spoon a little of the filling into the cannelloni and lay side by side in a well-buttered ovenproof dish. Spoon the sauce over the pasta to cover completely and sprinkle with the Parmesan cheese.

Bake, uncovered, in a moderately hot oven, 375°F, Gas Mark 5 for 20-30 minutes or until bubbling and golden.
Serves 4-6

TOMATO SAUCE (page 51)

Golden Cannelloni with Ham

8 tubes cannelloni
2 oz. (¼ cup) butter
2 oz. (½ cup) flour
½ pint (1¼ cups) milk
4 oz. (½ cup) ham, chopped
3 eggs, hard-boiled and chopped

salt and pepper
6 oz. (3 cups) fresh breadcrumbs
flour for coating
1 egg, beaten
oil for deep frying

Cook the tubes in boiling salted water until 'al dente'. Drain and keep in a bowl of cold water.

Melt the butter in a pan, stir in the flour and cook for 1 minute. Gradually pour in the milk and mix well. Bring to the boil, stirring continuously, and cook for 4 minutes. Add the ham, eggs, seasoning and half the breadcrumbs. Drain and dry the cannelloni, then carefully press the stuffing into each tube, and chill for 1 hour.

Roll each cannelloni in flour, dip in the beaten egg and coat evenly with the remaining breadcrumbs.

Deep fry the cannelloni until crisp and golden. Drain on kitchen paper and serve with a tomato sauce (see page 51).
Serves 2-4

Lasagne al Forno

1 lb. lasagne
1 quantity Bolognese sauce (see
  page 36)
2 oz. (½ cup) grated Parmesan
  cheese
Béchamel sauce:
2 oz. (¼ cup) butter

2 oz. (½ cup) plain (all-purpose)
  flour
1 pint (2½ cups) milk
salt
freshly ground black pepper
pinch of ground nutmeg

Cook the lasagne, a few at a time, in boiling salted water until 'al dente'. Drain them and place in a bowl of cold water.

To make the béchamel sauce, melt the butter in a pan, add the flour and mix to a paste. Remove from the heat and stir in the milk, salt, pepper and nutmeg. Bring to the boil, stirring constantly, and cook for 3 minutes.

Butter a deep ovenproof dish and spread some of the Bolognese sauce over the bottom, cover with a layer of the béchamel and then a layer of lasagne. Continue in this way until the dish is filled, finishing with the béchamel. Sprinkle generously with Parmesan cheese and bake in a moderate oven, 350°F, Gas Mark 4 for 30-40 minutes.
Serves 4-6

Meatballs with Linguine

1 lb. minced (ground) pork
1 clove garlic, crushed
2 tablespoons chopped fresh parsley
1 large slice white bread, soaked in
  a little milk
1 egg

salt and pepper
oil for frying
1 pint (2½ cups) tomato sauce (see
  page 51)
1 lb. linguine
1 oz. (2 T) butter

Place the pork, garlic and parsley in a bowl. Add the bread, egg and salt and pepper to taste and stir the mixture until thoroughly mixed. Using floured hands roll the pork mixture into small balls and fry in hot oil until golden brown. Drain on kitchen paper.

Heat the tomato sauce in a pan, add the meatballs and simmer very gently for 20 minutes or until cooked through.

Meanwhile, cook the linguine in a large pan of boiling salted water for 10-12 minutes or until 'al dente'. Drain thoroughly and place in a warm serving dish. Add the butter and toss well until melted. Pour the sauce and meatballs on top and serve immediately.
Serves 4

Noodle Bake

2 tablespoons olive oil
1 onion, chopped
1 clove garlic, crushed
1 green pepper, seeded and chopped
1 lb. (2 cups) minced (ground)
  pork
1 × 14 oz. can tomatoes
2 teaspoons chopped fresh oregano

salt
freshly ground black pepper
12 oz. tagliatelle
½ oz. (1 T) butter, cut into small
  pieces
½ oz. (¼ cup) Cheddar cheese,
  grated

Heat the oil in a saucepan and fry the onion, garlic and pepper for 5 minutes. Add the pork and fry until it loses its pinkness. Stir in the tomatoes, with the can juice, the oregano and salt and pepper to taste. Bring to the boil, cover and simmer for 30 minutes.

Meanwhile, cook the tagliatelle in boiling salted water until 'al dente'. Drain well. Spoon one-third of the meat mixture into a buttered ovenproof dish and top with half the tagliatelle. Continue making layers until all the ingredients are used up. Sprinkle over the butter and grated cheese and bake in a moderate oven, 350°F, Gas Mark 4 for 30 minutes, or until the top is brown and bubbly.
Serves 4-6

Tagliatelle with Mushroom and Bacon Sauce

3 tablespoons oil
4 oz. (6 slices) bacon, diced
8 oz. (2 cups) mushrooms, sliced
1 clove garlic, crushed
4 tomatoes, peeled and chopped
1 tablespoon chopped fresh parsley

½ teaspoon dried oregano
salt
freshly ground black pepper
1 lb. tagliatelle
1 oz. (¼ cup) grated Parmesan
  cheese

Heat the oil in a pan and cook the bacon until crisp. Add the mushrooms and cook for 5 minutes, then add the garlic, tomatoes and herbs. Season with salt and pepper and continue to cook for a further 5 minutes.

Cook the tagliatelle in boiling salted water until 'al dente', then drain and mix with the mushroom mixture and the cheese. Stir once and transfer to a heated serving dish.
Serves 4-6

TAGLIATELLE
(Photograph: Pasta Foods Limited)

Tagliatelle with Chicken Livers

3 tablespoons oil
1 onion, chopped
1 clove garlic, crushed
12 oz. (1½ cups) chicken livers,
  chopped
1 tablespoon chopped fresh parsley
1 tablespoon chopped fresh
  marjoram and thyme

6 oz. (1½ cups) mushrooms, sliced
¼ pint (⅔ cup) red wine
¼ pint (⅔ cup) stock
salt and pepper
1 lb. tagliatelle

Heat the oil in a saucepan and fry the onion and garlic for 5 minutes until soft. Add the livers, herbs and mushrooms and fry until the livers are lightly browned. Add the wine and stock and season well. Bring to the boil, stirring, then cover the pan and simmer for 15 minutes.

Meanwhile, cook the tagliatelle in a large pan of boiling salted water for 10-12 minutes or until 'al dente'. Drain thoroughly and transfer to a warm serving dish. Add the sauce, toss well and serve immediately.
Serves 4

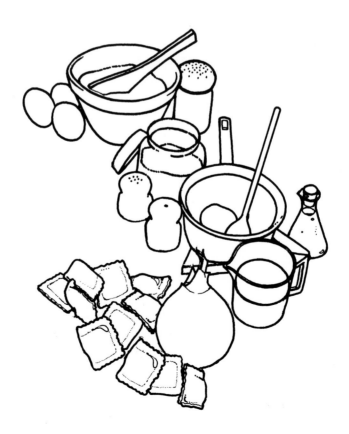

Ravioli with Meat Filling

Ravioli paste:
8 oz. (2 cups) plain (all-purpose)
  flour
1/4 teaspoon salt
2 oz. (1/4 cup) butter
8 fl. oz. (1 cup) boiling water

Filling:
2 tablespoons oil
1 small onion, chopped
1 clove garlic, crushed
4 oz. (1/2 cup) minced (ground)
  beef
1/4 pint (2/3 cup) red wine

1 tablespoon grated Parmesan
  cheese
1 tablespoon chopped fresh parlsey
1 tablespoon fresh breadcrumbs
4 oz. (1/2 cup) cooked chopped
  spinach
salt
freshly ground black pepper

To finish:
2 oz. (1/4 cup) butter, melted
1 oz. (1/4 cup) grated Parmesan
  cheese

Make the paste as for Ravioli with Ricotta and Spinach (see page 64), roll out and set aside while making the filling.

Heat the oil in a pan and fry the onion until transparent. Add the garlic and beef and brown well, then add the wine and simmer, covered, for 15 minutes. Mix in the remaining ingredients and use to fill the ravioli as in the recipe on page 64.

Slide the ravioli into boiling salted water and cook gently for about 6 minutes, until they rise to the top. Lift out carefully with a draining spoon and place in a heated serving dish. Pour over the melted butter and sprinkle with Parmesan cheese. Alternatively, serve with a tomato sauce (see page 51).

Serves 4

Farfalle with Mushrooms

4 tablespoons (¼ cup) oil
12 oz. (1½ cups) minced (ground)
  pork
2 cloves garlic, crushed
1 tablespoon flour
8 fl. oz. (1 cup) stock
4 fl. oz. (½ cup) white wine
2 tablespoons tomato purée

½ teaspoon dried basil
½ teaspoon dried oregano
salt
freshly ground black pepper
12 oz. (3 cups) button mushrooms,
  sliced
12 oz. (6 cups) farfalle
grated Parmesan cheese to serve

Heat 2 tablespoons of the oil in a pan, add the pork and allow to brown, stirring occasionally. Add the garlic and cook for a further 2 minutes. Stir in the flour, then add the stock, wine, tomato purée, basil, oregano and salt and pepper. Bring to the boil and simmer gently for 25 minutes. Sauté the mushrooms in the remaining oil, add to the meat mixture and simmer for a further 5 minutes.

Cook the farfalle in boiling salted water until 'al dente', then drain. Mix the meat mixture with the farfalle and serve immediately.

Hand grated Parmesan cheese separately.
Serves 4

FARFALLE WITH MUSHROOMS
(Photograph: Mushroom Growers' Association)

Macaroni with Frankfurters

8 oz. (2 cups) short cut macaroni
8 frankfurter sausages
1 × 7 oz. can sweetcorn kernels,
  drained
¾ pint (2 cups) hot mornay sauce
  (see below)

2 spring onions (scallions), chopped
1 oz. (¼ cup) Cheddar cheese,
  grated

Cook the macaroni in boiling salted water until 'al dente'.

Meanwhile, cook the frankfurters in boiling water according to the instructions on the packet. Drain the frankfurters and cut them into 1 inch pieces.

Drain the macaroni and return to the saucepan. Stir in the frankfurter pieces and corn, then fold in the hot sauce and the spring onions (scallions). Spoon into a flameproof serving dish. Sprinkle the cheese on top and place under a hot grill (broiler) until the top is lightly browned and bubbling.
Serves 4

Mornay Sauce

¾ pint (2 cups) milk
1 bay leaf
6 black peppercorns
slice of onion
1 mace blade
1½ oz. (3 T) butter
1½ oz. (⅓ cup) plain
  (all-purpose) flour

salt
freshly ground black pepper
2 teaspoons French mustard
8 oz. (2 cups) Cheddar cheese,
  grated

Put the milk, bay leaf, peppercorns, onion and mace blade in a saucepan and bring to just under boiling point. Remove from the heat, cover and leave to infuse for 10 minutes. Strain the milk.

Melt the butter in a saucepan. Add the flour and cook, stirring, for 1 minute. Remove from the heat and gradually stir in the hot strained milk. Return to the heat and bring to the boil, stirring. Simmer for 1 to 2 minutes or until thickened and smooth. Add salt and pepper to taste, the mustard and cheese. Stir until the cheese has melted.

Tomato Sauce

2 tablespoons olive oil
1 onion, chopped
1 stick celery, chopped
1 clove garlic, crushed
1½ lb. (3 cups) tomatoes, peeled,
  seeded and chopped

salt
freshly ground black pepper
pinch of sugar

Heat the oil in a pan and fry the onion and celery for 5 minutes. Add the garlic, tomatoes, salt, pepper and sugar. Simmer for 15-20 minutes until pulpy, then pass through a sieve (strainer) or purée in a blender. Serve with ravioli, cannelloni or other pasta.

Tomato and Ham Sauce

2 tablespoons oil
1 onion, chopped
4 oz. (1 cup) mushrooms, chopped
1 × 14 oz. can tomatoes, chopped
1 tablespoon tomato purée

¼ pint (⅔ cup) red wine
4 oz. (½ cup) cooked ham,
  chopped
salt
freshly ground black pepper

Heat the oil in a pan and fry the onion until transparent. Add the mushrooms and cook for a further 5 minutes, then add the remaining ingredients and simmer gently for 15 minutes. Pour over warm ravioli or other pasta and serve immediately.

FISH

Spaghetti with Tomato and Mussel Sauce

5 pints (6 pints) mussels
½ pint (1¼ cups) water
3 tablespoons olive oil
2 onions, chopped
2 cloves garlic, crushed
2 tablespoons chopped fresh parsley

½ teaspoon dried basil
½ teaspoon dried marjoram
2 lb. (4 cups) tomatoes, peeled and
  chopped
salt and pepper
1 lb. spaghetti

Clean the mussels, scrub well and remove the beards. Discard any mussels that do not close when tapped. Rinse thoroughly to remove any grit. Place the mussels in a large saucepan, add the water and bring to the boil. Cook for 4-5 minutes, shaking occasionally, until the shells open. Discard any that do not open. Drain the mussels and discard most of the shells, reserving a few in the shells for a garnish.

Heat the oil in a pan, add the onions and garlic and cook for 5 minutes or until soft. Add the herbs, tomatoes and salt and pepper to taste, bring to the boil and simmer for 15 minutes or until reduced to a pulp. Add the mussels and heat through for a few minutes.

Cook the spaghetti in a large pan of boiling salted water for 10-12 minutes or until 'al dente'. Drain and place in a warm serving dish. Pour over the mussel sauce and garnish with the reserved mussels. If liked, sprinkle with extra chopped parsley.

Spaghetti with Sardines

3 tablespoons olive oil
1 onion, chopped
1 lb. (2 cups) tomatoes, peeled and
  chopped
1 clove garlic, crushed
½ teaspoon saffron, soaked in 4
  tablespoons (¼ cup) boiling water

salt and pepper
1 × 4¾ oz. can sardines in brine
1 oz. (¼ cup) pine nuts
1 lb. spaghetti

Heat the oil in a pan and fry the onion until soft. Add the tomatoes, garlic, saffron water, seasoning to taste, sardines and pine nuts and simmer gently for 20 minutes.

Cook the spaghetti in a large pan of boiling salted water until 'al dente'. Drain and mix with the sardine sauce. Serve immediately.
Serves 4-6

Spaghetti with Clams

40 fresh clams
¼ pint (⅔ cup) dry white wine
2 tablespoons oil
1 onion, chopped
2 cloves garlic, crushed
1½ lb. (3 cups) tomatoes, peeled
  and chopped

2 tablespoons chopped fresh basil
salt
freshly ground black pepper
1 lb. spaghetti

Clean the clams by scrubbing well with a brush and rinsing under running water to remove all sand and grit. Discard any that will not close when tapped. Place the clams in a pan, pour over the wine, cover and cook for 5 minutes or until the shells open. Strain and remove from the shells. Discard any that do not open.

Heat the oil in a pan and cook the onion and garlic for 2 minutes. Stir in the tomatoes and simmer gently for 10 minutes. Add the clams, basil, salt and pepper and heat the fish for 5 minutes.

Cook the spaghetti in boiling salted water until 'al dente', then drain and place in a heated serving dish. Pour over the sauce and serve immediately.
Serves 4-6

Spaghetti with Smoked Fish

1 lb. smoked haddock
12 oz. spaghetti
2 oz. (¼ cup) butter
2 tablespoons chopped fresh parsley

salt and pepper
3 eggs, beaten
juice of ½ lemon

Poach the fish for 12-15 minutes or until cooked. Drain, flake the flesh and keep warm.

Cook the spaghetti in boiling salted water until 'al dente' and drain. Return to the pan with the flaked fish, butter, parsley and seasoning to taste. Cook, stirring, until hot, then stir in the beaten eggs.

Turn into a heated dish, sprinkle with lemon juice and serve immediately.
Serves 4

Spaghetti with Tuna Fish

2 tablespoons olive oil
1 clove garlic, chopped
6 oz. (1 cup) tuna, coarsely
  chopped
3 tablespoons chopped fresh parsley

2 tablespoons tomato purée
8 fl. oz. (1 cup) stock
salt
freshly ground black pepper
1 lb. spaghetti

Heat the oil and fry the garlic for 1 minute. Add the tuna fish, 2 tablespoons parsley, tomato purée and stock, and season with salt and pepper. Simmer gently for 15 minutes.

Cook the spaghetti in boiling salted water until 'al dente'. Drain, mix with the tuna sauce and sprinkle with the remaining chopped parsley.
Serves 4

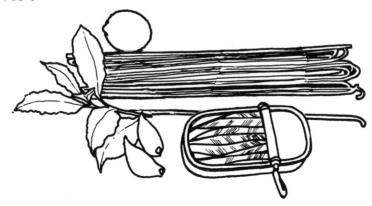

Fettuccine with Prawn (Shrimp) Sauce

4 tablespoons (¼ cup) olive oil
1 onion, chopped
2 cloves garlic, crushed
1 lb. (2 cups) tomatoes, peeled and
  chopped
½ teaspoon dried basil
salt

freshly ground black pepper
12 oz. (2 cups) peeled prawns
  (shelled shrimp)
¼ pint (⅔ cup) white wine
2 tablespoons chopped fresh parsley
1 lb. fettuccine
knob of butter to serve

Heat the oil in a pan and fry the onion and garlic until transparent. Add the tomatoes, basil, salt and pepper and simmer gently for 5 minutes. Stir in the prawns (shrimp), wine and parsley and simmer for a further 10 minutes.

Cook the fettuccine in boiling salted water until 'al dente'. Drain and place on a hot serving dish. Pour over the prawn (shrimp) sauce and serve with a knob of butter.
Serves 4-6

Fettucce with Anchovies

3 tablespoons oil
1 onion, chopped
1 clove garlic, crushed
1 × 2 oz. can anchovies, drained
  and chopped
2 tablespoons chopped fresh parsley
1 tablespoon chopped fresh fennel

1 × 14 oz. can tomatoes
1 oz. (3 T) sultanas (seedless white
  raisins)
salt
freshly ground black pepper
1 lb. fettucce

Heat the oil in a pan and fry the onion and garlic for 1 minute. Add the remaining ingredients, except the fettucce, and simmer uncovered for 20 minutes, stirring occasionally.

Cook the fettucce in boiling salted water until 'al dente'. Drain thoroughly and mix with the anchovy sauce.
Serves 6

SPAGHETTI WITH SMOKED FISH *(page 55)*
(Photograph: Pasta Information Centre)

Pasta with Tuna and Prawns (Shrimp)

2 tablespoons oil
1 onion, chopped
1 clove garlic, crushed
1 × 7½ oz. can tuna, drained
4 oz. (⅔ cup) peeled prawns
  (shelled shrimp)
8 fl. oz. (1 cup) single (light)
  cream
grated rind of ½ lemon
salt
freshly ground black pepper
12 oz. (3 cups) medium pasta
  shells
Garnish:
unpeeled prawns (unshelled
  shrimp)
fresh parsley sprigs

Heat the oil in a pan and cook the onion and garlic until transparent.
Add the tuna fish, prawns (shrimp), cream, lemon rind, salt and
pepper and heat gently for 5–10 minutes.

Cook the pasta shells in boiling, salted water until 'al dente'. Drain
and mix with the sauce. Serve garnished with the whole prawns
(shrimp) and parsley.
Serves 4

Fish and Pasta Florentine

1½ oz. (3 T) butter
1½ oz. (⅓ cup) flour
¾ pint (2 cups) milk
4 oz. (1 cup) medium pasta shells
2 eggs, hard-boiled and chopped
6 oz. (¾ cup) cooked smoked
  haddock, flaked
2 oz. (⅓ cup) peeled prawns
  (shelled shrimp)
salt and pepper
1½ lb. (3 cups) cooked spinach,
  chopped
2 oz. (½ cup) grated Parmesan
  cheese

Melt the butter in a pan, add the flour and cook for 1 minute.
Gradually stir in the milk and mix until smooth. Bring to the boil,
stirring constantly, and cook for 3 minutes.

Cook the pasta in a large pan of boiling salted water until 'al
dente'. Drain the pasta and mix with the sauce, eggs, fish, prawns
(shrimp) and seasoning. Spoon half the mixture into small ovenproof
dishes, top with the spinach, then with the remaining pasta and fish
mixture. Sprinkle over the cheese and bake in a moderately hot oven,
375°F, Gas Mark 5 for 30 minutes or until golden and bubbling.
Serves 4-6

VEGETABLES

Tripoline Syracuse Style

4 tablespoons (¼ cup) olive oil
1 large onion, sliced
2 cloves garlic, crushed
1 lb. courgettes (zucchini), chopped
1 green pepper, seeded and chopped
1 × 14 oz. can tomatoes, drained
  and roughly chopped
4 oz. (¾ cup) black olives, stoned
  (pitted)

3 anchovy fillets, finely chopped
1 tablespoon chopped fresh parsley
2 teaspoons chopped fresh or
  ½ teaspoon dried marjoram
salt and pepper
1 lb. tripoline
2 oz. (½ cup) grated Parmesan
  cheese

Heat the oil in a saucepan, add the onion and garlic and fry for 5
minutes or until soft. Add the courgettes (zucchini) and fry for 10
minutes. Add the pepper, tomatoes, olives, anchovies, parsley,
marjoram and salt and pepper to taste. Bring to the boil, stirring.
Cover the pan and simmer while cooking the tripoline.

Cook the tripoline in a large pan of boiling salted water for 10-12
minutes or until 'al dente'. Drain well and place in a hot serving dish.
Add the cheese and the sauce and toss lightly together. Serve
immediately.
Serves 4

Spaghetti with Aubergine (Eggplant) and Tomato Sauce

1 tablespoon oil
1 large onion, sliced
1 clove garlic, crushed
1 aubergine (eggplant), chopped
1 green pepper, seeded and diced
1 × 15 oz. can tomatoes
1 wineglass red wine
½ teaspoon dried basil

½ teaspoon dried oregano
salt
freshly ground black pepper
4 oz. (1 cup) button mushrooms,
 sliced
1 tablespoon tomato purée
1 lb. spaghetti
grated Parmesan cheese to serve

Heat the oil in a pan and fry the onion and garlic until softened. Add the aubergine (eggplant), pepper, tomatoes, wine, herbs, salt and pepper, bring to the boil and cook for 30 minutes. Stir in the mushrooms and tomato purée and cook for a further 5 minutes.

Cook the spaghetti in boiling salted water for 10-15 minutes, until 'al dente'. Drain well and place on a heated serving dish. Pour over the sauce and serve with Parmesan cheese handed separately.
Serves 4

Spaghetti with Tomato Sauce and Olives

1 pint (2½ cups) tomato sauce (see
 page 51)
1 lb. spaghetti
2 tablespoons olive oil
8 oz. (1½ cups) black olives,
 stoned (pitted)

2 tablespoons chopped fresh parsley
1 oz. (¼ cup) grated Parmesan
 cheese

Prepare the tomato sauce. Cook the spaghetti in a large pan of boiling salted water for 10-12 minutes or until 'al dente'. Drain well.

Meanwhile, heat the oil in a pan, add the olives and parsley and heat through.

Place the spaghetti in a warm serving bowl, pour over the sauce and the olive mixture and toss well. Sprinkle with Parmesan cheese and serve immediately.
Serves 6

SPAGHETTI WITH AUBERGINE (EGGPLANT) AND TOMATO SAUCE
(Photograph: Carmel Produce Information Bureau)

Fettuccine with Pesto

1 lb. fettuccine
knob of butter
Pesto:
2 cloves garlic, chopped
6 tablespoons chopped fresh basil
1 oz. (¼ cup) pine nuts

1 oz. (¼ cup) grated Parmesan or
  Pecorino cheese
3 tablespoons olive oil
salt
freshly ground black pepper

Pound the garlic, basil, pine nuts and cheese in a mortar until smooth. Gradually add the olive oil until the sauce is thick and creamy. Season with salt and pepper to taste.

Cook the fettuccine in boiling salted water until 'al dente', drain and place on a heated serving dish. Spoon the pesto sauce over the fettuccine and top with the knob of butter. Serve with additional grated Parmesan or Pecorino cheese.
Serves 4

Tagliatelle Riviera

3 tablespoons olive oil
2 onions, sliced
2 cloves garlic, crushed
2 slices lean bacon, rinds removed
  and chopped
8 oz. (2 cups) mushrooms, sliced
2 anchovy fillets, chopped

6 black olives, halved and stoned
  (pitted)
salt
freshly ground black pepper
1 lb. tagliatelle
1 oz. (¼ cup) grated Parmesan
  cheese

Heat the oil in a frying pan (skillet). Add the onions, garlic and bacon and fry until the onions are soft but not brown. Stir in the mushrooms, anchovy fillets, olives and salt and pepper to taste. Cook for a further 4–5 minutes or until very hot.

Meanwhile cook the tagliatelle in boiling salted water until it is 'al dente'. Drain the tagliatelle and arrange in a warmed serving dish. Spoon over the sauce and sprinkle with the Parmesan cheese.
Serves 4

Cauliflower and Spaghetti Soufflé

1 small cauliflower, divided into
  florets
4 oz. (1 cup) spaghetti, broken into
  short pieces
1 oz. (2 T) butter
2 tablespoons flour
½ pint (1¼ cups) milk

4 oz. (1 cup) grated Parmesan
  cheese
salt
cayenne pepper
dry mustard
5 eggs, separated

Cook the cauliflower in boiling salted water until tender. Drain well and mash to a purée. Meanwhile, cook the spaghetti in boiling salted water until 'al dente'. Drain well.

Melt the butter in a pan, stir in the flour, then remove from the heat and add the milk. Return to the heat and cook, stirring constantly, for 2-3 minutes until thickened and smooth. Stir in the Parmesan cheese and season well with salt, cayenne pepper and mustard. Add the egg yolks one at a time, beating well, then mix in the spaghetti and the cauliflower purée.

Whisk the egg whites until stiff, but not dry, and fold gently into the spaghetti mixture. Pour into a greased and lined 3 pint (7½ cup) soufflé dish and cook in a moderately hot oven, 375°F, Gas Mark 5 for 30-35 minutes until golden. Serve immediately.
Serves 8

Linguine with Tomato and Garlic

3 tablespoons olive oil
2 lb. (4 cups) tomatoes, peeled and
  chopped
3 cloves garlic, crushed
½ teaspoon dried oregano

1 tablespoon chopped fresh parsley
salt
freshly ground black pepper
1 lb. linguine
grated Parmesan cheese to serve

Heat the oil in a pan and cook the tomatoes and garlic together for 3-4 minutes. Add the oregano, parsley, salt and pepper and cook for a further few minutes.

Cook the linguine in boiling salted water until 'al dente'. Drain thoroughly and mix with the sauce. Transfer to a heated dish and serve with grated Parmesan cheese.
Serves 4-6

Ravioli with Spinach and Ricotta Filling

Ravioli Paste:
8 oz. (2 cups) plain (all-purpose)
 flour
¼ teaspoon salt
2 oz. (¼ cup) butter
8 fl. oz. (1 cup) boiling water
Filling:
4 oz. (½ cup) cooked spinach
 purée, drained

3 oz. (½ cup) Ricotta cheese
1 oz. (¼ cup) grated Parmesan
 cheese
pinch of ground nutmeg
salt
freshly ground black pepper
1 egg yolk

Sift the flour and salt into a bowl and rub in the butter with the fingertips, until it resembles fine breadcrumbs. Add sufficient water to make a stiff dough; knead until smooth, then divide the dough in half. Roll out one piece of dough as thin as you can make it without breaking it; set aside and cover with a cloth to prevent it drying out. Roll out the other half of the dough to the same size, flouring constantly to prevent it sticking, and turning frequently. Set aside and cover with a cloth.

To make the filling, mix the spinach, cheeses, nutmeg, salt and pepper together and bind with the egg yolk.

Brush one sheet of the paste with cold water. Using a teaspoon, place small heaps of the filling over the paste, about 1½ inches apart. Cover with the second sheet of paste, allowing it to lie loosely, not stretched, over the filling. Press down round each mound of filling and cut with a pastry wheel or small fluted cutter. Transfer the ravioli to a floured tray and leave to dry for 30 minutes.

Slide the ravioli into boiling salted water and cook them gently for about 6 minutes, until they rise to the top. Lift out carefully with a draining spoon and place in a heated serving dish. Serve with tomato and ham sauce (see page 51).
Serves 4

RAVIOLI WITH SPINACH AND RICOTTA FILLING
(Photograph: Pasta Information Centre)

Stuffed Tomatoes

2 oz. (½ cup) miniature pasta
8 large tomatoes
4 spring onions (scallions), chopped
4 oz. (½ cup) cooked chicken,
  diced
2 caps red pimiento, diced

salt
freshly ground black pepper
3 tablespoons mayonnaise
1 tablespoon curry sauce
2 tablespoons double (heavy) cream

Cook the pasta in boiling salted water until 'al dente', then rinse and drain well.

Cut the tops off the tomatoes and scoop out the seeds. Mix the pasta, spring onions (scallions), chicken and pimiento in a bowl. Add salt and pepper to taste. Mix the mayonnaise with the curry sauce and cream, then spoon onto the pasta mixture. Stir thoroughly and use to fill the tomato shells. Replace the tops and serve.
Serves 4

Spaghetti with Broccoli and Pine Nuts

8 oz. broccoli
2 tablespoons olive oil
1 onion, finely chopped
1 clove garlic, crushed
1 oz. (¼ cup) pine nuts, chopped

salt
freshly ground black pepper
1 × 12 oz. packet wholewheat
  spaghetti

Steam the broccoli gently in boiling salted water for 10 minutes. Drain and chop finely.

Heat the oil in a frying pan (skillet) and fry the onion and garlic until transparent. Add the chopped broccoli, pine nuts and salt and pepper to taste. Stir thoroughly and keep hot.

Cook the spaghetti as directed on the packet. When cooked, drain and mix with the broccoli and pine nut mixture. Pile onto a heated serving dish and serve immediately.
Serves 4

Vegetable Lasagne

12 oz. lasagne

6 oz. Mozzarella cheese, thinly
  sliced

3 eggs, hard-boiled and sliced

4 oz. (1 cup) grated Parmesan
  cheese

8 oz. Ricotta cheese

Tomato Sauce:

3 lb. (6 cups) tomatoes, peeled and
  chopped

3 tablespoons tomato purée

2 carrots, chopped

1 onion, chopped

2 cloves garlic, crushed

2 sticks celery, chopped

1 tablespoon chopped fresh parsley

½ teaspoon grated lemon rind

Put all the sauce ingredients, into a large saucepan. Cover and
simmer for 45 minutes. Cool slightly then purée in a blender. Return
the purée to the rinsed-out pan and continue to simmer for 30
minutes or until thick.

  Meanwhile, cook the lasagne, a few at a time, in boiling salted
water for 15 minutes or until they are 'al dente'. Drain well and use
about one-third to line the bottom of a buttered baking dish. Cover
with half the Mozzarella and half the eggs. Sprinkle with one-third of
the Parmesan, then spread over half the Ricotta and half the sauce.
Continue making layers, finishing with a thick covering of Parmesan
cheese. Bake in a moderate oven, 350°F, Gas Mark 4 for 40 minutes.

Serves 6

Cannelloni with Tomato Stuffing

12 cannelloni tubes or 1 quantity of
egg pasta dough (see page 10), cut
into cannelloni
8 oz. (1 cup) tomatoes, peeled and
chopped
4 oz. (1 cup) cheese, grated
(preferably a mixture of Cheddar
and Parmesan)

4 oz. (2 cups) fresh breadcrumbs
salt
freshly ground black pepper
1 egg, lightly beaten
1 × 14 oz. can tomatoes
1 teaspoon dried basil

Cook the pasta in a large pan of boiling salted water until 'al dente'.
Lift out the pasta and lay on a cloth to drain.

Mix together the tomatoes, cheese, breadcrumbs, salt and pepper
to taste and the egg. Fill the cannelloni tubes with this mixture or
divide between the squares of homemade pasta and roll up. Place the
filled cannelloni in a buttered ovenproof dish. Mix together the
canned tomatoes, with the juice, and basil, stirring to break up the
tomatoes. Pour over the cannelloni. Bake in a moderate oven, 350°F,
Gas Mark 4 for 30 minutes.
Serves 4

SALADS

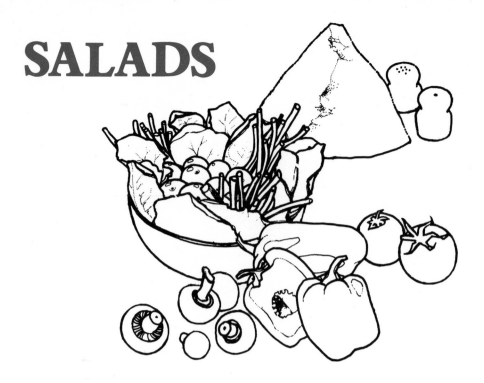

Curried Spaghetti and Mushroom Salad

12 oz. (3 cups) spaghetti, broken
  into short lengths
4 spring onions (scallions), chopped
2 sticks celery, chopped
6 oz. (1½ cups) button
  mushrooms, sliced
1 tablespoon chopped fresh parsley
lettuce leaves to serve

Dressing:
6 tablespoons olive oil
2 tablespoons wine vinegar
2 teaspoons curry powder
2 tablespoons tomato purée
1 teaspoon soft (light) brown sugar
salt
freshly ground black pepper

Cook the spaghetti in boiling salted water until 'al dente', then rinse
and drain. Make a dressing by whisking together the oil, vinegar,
curry powder, tomato purée, sugar, salt and pepper. Pour over the
spaghetti and mix well. Add the onions (scallions), celery,
mushrooms and parsley. Serve on a bed of lettuce.
Serves 6-8

Herring and Apple Salad

4 oz. (2 cups) large pasta shells
2 tablespoons French dressing
2 tablespoons raisins
2 red dessert apples, cored and
  thinly sliced
1 × 5 oz. carton (⅔ cup) soured
  cream

grated rind and juice of ½ lemon
salt and pepper
1 tablespoon chopped fresh parsley
4 rollmops, cut into pieces

Cook the pasta in a large pan of boiling salted water until 'al dente'. Rinse and drain. Mix with the French dressing, while warm, and stir in the raisins and apples.

Mix the soured cream with the lemon rind and juice, seasoning to taste, and parsley.

Place the pasta on a shallow serving dish and arrange the rollmops on top. Spoon over the sauce and serve.

Serves 4

Salami Pasta Salad

6 oz. (3 cups) large pasta shells
1 green pepper, seeded and chopped
4 spring onions (scallions), chopped
4 oz. (¾ cup) sweetcorn kernels
4 tomatoes, peeled, seeded and
  chopped

4 oz. (½ cup) salami, diced
4 tablespoons (¼ cup) mayonnaise
2 tablespoons single (light) cream
salt and pepper
watercress to garnish

Cook the pasta in a large pan of boiling, salted water until 'al dente'. Rinse and drain. Mix the pasta with the pepper, onions (scallions), sweetcorn, tomatoes and salami.

Combine the mayonnaise with the cream, season generously and pour over the salad. Toss well, serve in a salad bowl and garnish with the watercress.

Serves 4-6

Pasta with Avocado and Lemon Sauce

12 oz. (3 cups) medium pasta
  shells
2 tablespoons olive oil
4 spring onions (scallions), chopped
2 tablespoons chopped fresh parsley
few strips of thinly pared lemon
  rind (optional)

Sauce:
1 ripe avocado
juice of 1 lemon
1 clove garlic, crushed
1 teaspoon sugar
salt
freshly ground black pepper
¼ pint (⅔ cup) single (light)
  cream

Cook the pasta shells in boiling salted water until 'al dente', rinse and drain well. Mix with the oil and leave to cool.

Halve the avocado, remove the stone (pit) and scoop the flesh into a blender. Add the lemon juice, garlic, sugar, salt, pepper and cream and blend together until smooth. Mix the avocado and lemon sauce with the pasta and stir in the spring onions (scallions) and parsley. If liked, sprinkle with strips of lemon rind.
Serves 6-8

Italian Avocado Salad

6 oz. (1½ cups) medium pasta
  shells
2 sticks celery, diced
1 green pepper, seeded and diced
4 oz. (1 cup) button mushrooms,
  sliced
1 tablespoon chopped walnuts

1 tablespoon chopped fresh parsley
1 clove garlic, crushed
4 tablespoons (¼ cup) French
  dressing
1 avocado
lettuce to serve

Cook the pasta in a large pan of boiling salted water until 'al dente'. Rinse, drain and cool.

Put the pasta, celery, pepper, mushrooms, walnuts, parsley and garlic in a bowl, stir in the dressing and toss well. Remove the skin and stone (pit) from the avocado, chop the flesh coarsely and add to the salad. Toss well and arrange on a bed of lettuce. Serve immediately.
Serves 4-6

PASTA WITH AVOCADO AND LEMON SAUCE
(Photograph: Pasta Information Centre)

Chicken and Avocado Salad

6 oz. (3 cups) pasta shapes
1 tablespoon olive oil
1 large ripe avocado
4 fl. oz. (½ cup) French dressing

8 oz. (1 cup) cooked chicken, cut
  into strips
2 sticks celery, finely sliced
10 black olives, stoned (pitted)

Cook the pasta in boiling salted water until 'al dente', then rinse and drain. Mix with the oil and leave to cool.

Peel the avocado, cut into cubes and mix with the dressing. Turn the pasta into a bowl and mix with the chicken, celery and olives. Pour over the avocado and dressing mixture and toss lightly.

Serves 4-6

Ham and Melon Salad

6 oz. (3 cups) pasta bows
6 oz. ham
1 tablespoon finely chopped onion
4 sticks celery, chopped
1 tablespoon chopped fresh parsley
½ small honeydew melon

2 tablespoons mayonnaise
2 tablespoons single (light) cream
1 teaspoon creamed horseradish
1 teaspoon lemon juice
salt and pepper
watercress to garnish

Cook the pasta in a large pan of boiling salted water until 'al dente'. Rinse, drain and allow to cool.

Cut the ham into strips and add to the pasta with the onion, celery and parsley. Cut the melon into cubes and add to the salad. Combine the mayonnaise with the cream, horseradish, lemon juice and seasoning to taste. Pour over the salad and toss well. Place on a serving dish and garnish with the watercress.

Serves 4-6

Winter Salad

6 oz. (3 cups) pasta bows
6 oz. (¾ cup) cooked chicken,
  diced
2 sticks celery, diced
2 red apples, cored and diced
1 green pepper, seeded and diced

salt
freshly ground black pepper
6 tablespoons mayonnaise
2 oz. (½ cup) walnuts, roughly
  chopped

Cook the pasta in boiling salted water until 'al dente'. Drain well and leave to cool.

Mix the chicken with the celery, apples, pepper, pasta and seasoning. Fold in the mayonnaise, turn into a salad bowl and sprinkle with the walnuts.

Serves 4-6

Country Salad

8 oz. (2½ cups) pasta rings
1 tablespoon olive oil
4 tomatoes, peeled and chopped
1 green pepper, seeded and chopped
2 oz. (⅓ cup) stuffed olives, sliced
6 oz. (1½ cups) button
  mushrooms, sliced

salt
freshly ground black pepper
1 tablespoon tomato ketchup
6 tablespoons French dressing

Cook the pasta in boiling salted water until 'al dente'. Drain and mix
with the oil, then leave to cool.

Mix the pasta with the tomatoes, pepper, olives and mushrooms
and season with salt and pepper. Mix the tomato ketchup with the
French dressing and stir into the salad until evenly coated. Serve on a
bed of lettuce.
Serves 4-6

Provençale Pasta Salad

6 oz. (2 cups) pasta rings
4 fl. oz. (½ cup) French dressing
6 tomatoes, peeled, seeded and
  chopped
4 oz. French (green) beans, cooked
12 black olives, stoned (pitted)
1 × 7½ oz. can tuna, drained and
  flaked

salt
freshly ground black pepper
1 small head lettuce, shredded
1 × 2 oz. can anchovy fillets,
  drained, to garnish

Cook the pasta in boiling salted water until 'al dente'. Drain well and
mix with a little of the dressing. When cool, turn into a bowl and
mix with the tomatoes, beans, olives, flaked tuna and seasoning.

Toss the salad lightly in the remaining dressing and serve on a bed
of shredded lettuce garnished with the anchovies.
Serves 6

COUNTRY SALAD
(Photograph: Pasta Foods Limited)

Scandinavian Beetroot Salad

8 oz. (2 ½ cups) pasta rings
8 oz. (1 ⅓ cups) beetroot (beet),
  cooked, peeled and diced
4 spring onions (scallions), chopped
2 dill pickles, chopped
¼ pint (⅔ cup) double (heavy)
  cream, lightly whipped
1 teaspoon chopped fresh parsley to
  garnish

Dressing:
4 tablespoons (¼ cup) olive oil
1 tablespoon wine vinegar
1 clove garlic, crushed
salt
freshly ground black pepper
1 teaspoon chopped fresh parsley
1 teaspoon chopped fresh fennel

Cook the pasta in boiling salted water until 'al dente' then rinse and
drain well.

Make a dressing by whisking together the oil, vinegar, garlic, salt,
pepper and herbs, and mix with the pasta while still warm. When
cool, mix with the beetroot (beet), onions (scallions) and pickles, and
fold in the cream. Pile into a serving dish and garnish with the
parsley.
Serves 4-6

Courgette (Zucchini) and Pasta Salad

6 oz. (1 ½ cups) pasta shells
6 tablespoons French dressing
4 courgettes (zucchini), sliced
2 tomatoes, peeled and chopped
8 black olives, stoned (pitted)

2 spring onions (scallions), chopped
salt
freshly ground black pepper
1 tablespoon chopped fresh parsley

Cook the pasta in boiling salted water until 'al dente', then rinse and
drain well. While still warm, mix with the dressing.

Cook the courgettes (zucchini) in boiling salted water for 8
minutes until just tender, then drain and cool. Add to the pasta with
the tomatoes, olives, onions (scallions), salt, pepper and parsley. Mix
well and serve cold.
Serves 4

Macaroni and Mushroom Salad

8 oz. (2 cups) button mushrooms,
  sliced
4 tablespoons (¼ cup) lemon juice
2 tablespoons wine vinegar
1 clove garlic, crushed
salt
freshly ground black pepper
1 lb. (4 cups) macaroni, broken
  into short lengths

1 red pepper, seeded and chopped
1 green pepper, seeded and chopped
¼ pint (⅔ cup) mayonnaise
¼ pint (⅔ cup) natural
  (unflavored) yogurt
chopped fresh parsley to garnish

Place the mushrooms in a shallow dish and sprinkle over the lemon
juice, vinegar, garlic and salt and pepper. Fold together carefully and
leave to marinate for 30 minutes.

Meanwhile, cook the macaroni in boiling salted water until 'al
dente'. Rinse and drain thoroughly.

Stir the chopped peppers into the mushroom mixture. Mix together
the mayonnaise and yogurt and add to the mushroom mixture. Fold
in the macaroni and mix well. Chill lightly and serve garnished with
parsley.
Serves 6

Italian Salmon Salad

6 oz. (3 cups) pasta bows
1 × 7 oz. can salmon, drained and
 flaked
1 red pepper, seeded and finely
 diced

½ cucumber, finely diced
10 black olives, stoned (pitted)
4 fl. oz. (½ cup) French dressing
watercress to garnish

Cook the pasta in a large pan of boiling salted water until 'al dente'.
Drain thoroughly and leave to cool.

Mix the flaked salmon with the pepper, cucumber, olives and
pasta. Pour over the dressing and toss lightly. Arrange in a serving
dish and garnish with sprigs of watercress.
Serves 4-6

Melon and Prawn (Shrimp) Cocktail

4 oz. (1¼ cups) pasta wheels
2 tomatoes, peeled and cut into 8
 pieces
½ honeydew melon, cut into cubes
6 oz. (1 cup) peeled prawns
 (shelled shrimp)
½ cucumber, cut into cubes
cucumber slices to garnish

Dressing:
3 tablespoons mayonnaise
1 tablespoon tomato ketchup
3 tablespoons soured cream
salt
freshly ground black pepper

Cook the pasta in boiling salted water until 'al dente', then rinse and
drain well.

Mix the pasta, tomatoes, melon, prawns (shrimp) and cucumber
together in a bowl. Make a dressing by mixing the mayonnaise,
tomato ketchup, soured cream, salt and pepper. Pour the dressing
over the pasta mixture and toss well. Spoon into glasses and garnish
each one with a cucumber slice.
Serves 4-6

ITALIAN SALMON SALAD
(Photograph: Princes-Buitoni)

DESSERTS

Fudge Pudding

8 oz. (2 cups) egg noodles
4 oz. (½ cup) butter
3 tablespoons soft brown sugar
4 oz. marshmallows

2 tablespoons single (light) cream
vanilla essence (extract)
2 oz. (½ cup) walnuts, chopped

Cook the noodles in a large pan of boiling salted water until soft and
drain well.

Put the butter, sugar, marshmallows and cream into a pan and stir
over a gentle heat until melted. Add the vanilla to taste and the pasta
and heat through.

Serve immediately, sprinkled with walnuts.
Serves 4

Honey and Sesame Noodles

8 oz. (2 cups) egg noodles
2 oz. (¼ cup) butter
2 teaspoons sesame seeds
2 tablespoons sultanas (seedless
  white raisins)

3 tablespoons clear honey
pinch of cinnamon
1 × 5 oz. carton (⅔ cup) soured
  cream

Cook the noodles in a pan of boiling salted water until 'al dente' and
drain.

Heat the butter in a pan and fry the sesame seeds until golden. Add
the sultanas (raisins), honey, cinnamon and noodles and heat
through.

Serve immediately with the soured cream.
Serves 4

Apple and Sultana (Raisin) Layer

4 oz. (1 cup) egg noodles
1 oz. (2 T) butter
4 cooking apples, peeled, cored and
   sliced
2 tablespoons soft brown sugar
pinch of cinnamon
3 tablespoons sultanas (seedless
   white raisins)

2 egg yolks
1 tablespoon castor sugar
1 tablespoon cornflour (cornstarch)
½ pint (1¼ cups) milk
2 tablespoons flaked almonds

Cook the noodles in a large pan of boiling salted water until soft.
Drain.

Melt the butter in a pan, add the apples, sugar and cinnamon;
cover the pan and simmer gently until the apples are soft. Stir in the
sultanas (raisins) and set aside.

Beat the egg yolks, sugar and cornflour (cornstarch) together until
thick and creamy. Heat the milk and pour onto the egg mixture.
Cook the custard in the top of a double saucepan until it will coat the
back of a spoon.

Place half the noodles in a shallow ovenproof dish, spread the
apple mixture over the top and finish with the remaining noodles.
Pour over the custard, sprinkle with the almonds and bake in a
moderate oven, 350°F, Gas Mark 4 for 20 minutes.
Serves 4

Noodles Jubilee

8 oz. (2 cups) egg noodles
2 tablespoons clear honey
1 × 15 oz. can black cherries
2 teaspoons arrowroot

2 tablespoons brandy (optional)
2 oz. (½ cup) flaked almonds
   (optional)

Cook the noodles in boiling water until just tender. Drain, and stir in
the honey.

Blend a little of the cherry juice with the arrowroot. Drain the
remaining juice into a pan and bring to the boil. Thicken with the
blended arrowroot. Add the brandy (if using) and the cherries and
heat through. Stir into the cooked noodles and sprinkle with the
nuts, if liked. Serve with cream.
Serves 4

Vermicelli and Almond Pudding

8 oz. (2 cups) vermicelli
2 oz. (¼ cup) butter, cut into
  pieces
2 oz. (⅓ cup) sultanas (seedless
  white raisins)
1 oz. (3 T) chopped candied peel

3 oz. (¾ cup) flaked almonds
¼ teaspoon ground cinnamon
2 oz. (¼ cup) castor (superfine)
  sugar
2 eggs, beaten

Cook the vermicelli in boiling salted water until 'al dente', then drain well. Return the pasta to the pan with the butter, sultanas (white raisins), peel, 2 oz. (½ cup) of the almonds, and the cinnamon mixed with the sugar. Add the eggs, mix well and pour into a buttered ovenproof dish. Sprinkle the remaining almonds over the top and bake in a moderate oven, 350°F, Gas Mark 4 for 30 minutes.
  Serve hot, with whipped cream.
Serves 4

Strawberry Mould

1 pint (2½ cups) milk
2 oz. (¼ cup) small pasta shells
1½ oz. (3 T) castor sugar
vanilla essence (extract)
½ oz. (1 envelope unflavored)
  gelatine

4 tablespoons (¼ cup) orange juice
4 fl. oz. (½ cup) double (heavy)
  cream, whipped
8 oz. (1½ cups) strawberries
1 egg white

Place the milk and pasta in a pan and bring to the boil, stirring constantly. Cover and simmer gently for 30 minutes or until tender. Add the sugar and vanilla to taste and leave to cool.
  Sprinkle the gelatine over the orange juice in a small bowl; place in a pan of hot water and heat gently until dissolved. Stir into the pasta mixture. Fold in the cream and 6 oz. (1¼ cups) of the strawberries, cut into quarters.
  Whisk the egg white until stiff, fold into the pasta cream and turn into an oiled 1½ pint (3¾ cup) mould. Place in the refrigerator to set. Turn out onto a serving dish and decorate with the remaining strawberries.
Serves 4

NOODLES JUBILEE (page 83)
(Photograph: Pasta Information Centre)

Apricot Creams

3 oz. (⅓ cup) miniature pasta
  shapes
1 pint (2½ cups) milk
2 tablespoons sugar
vanilla essence (extract)

1 × 7½ oz. can apricots
¼ pint (⅔ cup) double (heavy)
  cream
sponge fingers (ladyfingers) to serve

Place the pasta and milk in a pan and bring to the boil, stirring, and simmer gently for 30 minutes or until the pasta is soft, adding more milk if necessary. Add the sugar and vanilla to taste and allow to cool.

Drain the apricots, reserving a few for decoration. Chop the remainder.

Whisk the cream until thick and fold carefully into the pasta. Fold in the chopped apricots and pour into individual glasses. Decorate with the reserved apricots and serve with sponge fingers.
Serves 4

Baked Macaroni with Apricots

4 oz. (1 cup) short cut macaroni
1 pint (2½ cups) milk
½ pint (1¼ cups) single (light)
  cream
2 oz. (⅓ cup) soft brown sugar
4 oz. (½ cup) dried apricots,
  soaked overnight, drained and
  chopped

2 oz. (⅓ cup) sultanas (seedless
  white raisins)
pinch of ground nutmeg

Place the macaroni, milk and cream in a pan and bring to the boil,
stirring. Cover and simmer gently for 40 minutes, stirring
occasionally, until very soft. Add the sugar, apricots and sultanas
(white raisins), mix well and turn into a buttered, 2 pint (5 cup)
ovenproof dish. Sprinkle with nutmeg and bake in a moderate oven,
325°F, Gas Mark 3 for 30 minutes. Serve hot or cold.
Serves 4

Orange Macaroni Dessert

8 oz. (2 cups) short cut macaroni
2 oranges
¼ pint (⅔ cup) single (light)
  cream

8 oz. (1 cup) cream cheese
½ teaspoon ground cinnamon
2 tablespoons flaked almonds,
  toasted

Cook the macaroni in boiling salted water for 15 minutes until soft,
then drain well and cool slightly.

Grate the zest from 1 orange and set aside. Peel both oranges and
divide them into segments. Mix the cream, cream cheese, orange zest
and cinnamon together, and fold into the macaroni with the orange
segments. Spoon into glasses and sprinkle with the almonds.
Serves 6–8

Pasta Melba

2 pints (5 cups) milk
4 oz. (1 cup) short cut pasta
1 oz. (¼ cup) cornflour
  (cornstarch)
¼ pint (⅔ cup) double (heavy)
  cream, whipped

sugar to taste
2 tablespoons brandy
3 fresh peaches, skinned
6 scoops vanilla ice cream
6 tablespoons raspberry jam, heated

Bring the milk to the boil, add the pasta and simmer gently for 15 minutes, stirring occasionally. Mix the cornflour (cornstarch) with a little extra milk, add to the pan and cook until thick and smooth, stirring constantly. Leave to cool.

When cool, fold in the cream, sugar and brandy, and spoon into six sundae glasses. Halve the peaches and place one half in each glass, top with a scoop of ice cream and raspberry jam.
Serves 6

Banana and Pasta Caramel

5 oz. (1¼ cups) short cut pasta
4 egg yolks
3 tablespoons castor sugar
2 tablespoons cornflour (cornstarch)
½ pint (1¼ cups) milk

½ pint (1¼ cups) single (light)
  cream
3-4 bananas, sliced
4 oz. (⅔ cup) demerara (brown)
  sugar

Cook the pasta in a large pan of boiling salted water until tender. Drain.

Beat the egg yolks, sugar and cornflour (cornstarch) together until thick and creamy. Heat the milk and cream until hot and pour onto the egg mixture. Pour the custard mixture into the top of a double saucepan and stir over a moderate heat until the custard will coat the back of a spoon. Stir in the cooked pasta and pour into a shallow ovenproof dish. Allow to cool.

Top with slices of banana and completely coat with the demerara (brown) sugar. Place under a very hot grill (broiler) until the sugar caramelizes. Cool and chill before serving.
Serves 6-8

PASTA MELBA
(Photograph: Pasta Information Centre)

Caramelized Peaches with Pasta

1 pint (2½ cups) milk
3 oz. (¾ cup) short cut macaroni
vanilla essence (extract)
1 tablespoon castor sugar
1 egg

1 × 15 oz. can peach halves,
  drained
3 tablespoons soft brown sugar
whipped cream to serve

Place the milk and pasta in a pan and bring to the boil, stirring.
Cover and simmer gently for 30-40 minutes or until the pasta is soft,
adding more milk if necessary. Cool slightly, then add the vanilla to
taste, sugar and egg and mix well. Cook over a very gentle heat for 1
minute to thicken the egg, stirring continuously.

Turn into a buttered, flameproof dish, arrange the peaches on top
and sprinkle with the brown sugar. Place under a hot grill (broiler) to
caramelize the sugar. Serve hot with whipped cream.
Serves 4

INDEX

INDEX